UNICORNS
AMONG US

Understanding The High Priests Of
Data Science

Unicorns Among Us

Understanding The High Priests Of Data Science

Lars Nielsen

New Street Communications, LLC

Wickford, Rhode Island

newstreetcommunications.com

Published 2014 by
New Street Communications, LLC
Wickford, Rhode Island

newstreetcommunications.com

You may also enjoy Lars Nielsen's ...

A Simple Introduction to Data Science

Computing: A Business History

Contents

1
High Priests

There are only patterns, patterns on top of patterns, patterns that affect other patterns. Patterns hidden by patterns. Patterns within patterns. ... What we call chaos is just patterns we haven't recognized. What we call random is just patterns we can't decipher. What we can't understand we call nonsense. What we can't read we call gibberish.
- Chuck Palahniuk

The profession of data scientist didn't even exist in the first few years of the 21st century. (Actually, the term *data science* itself wasn't even coined until 2008, when D.J. Patil, and Jeff Hammerbacher, then the respective leads of data and analytics for LinkedIn and Facebook, came up with it.) But now, midway into the second decade of the century, data science and those who practice it comprise one of the fastest growing and most lucrative corners of the digital labor market. Financial institutions, retail sellers, social media enterprises, and just about every other industry all need the data scientist to derive actionable business intelligence (or BI) from the tidal wave of big data with which they are both blessed and swamped – all those ad clicks and digital purchases and likes and other hints and records of consumer behavior.

These data scientists – the so-called *high-priests* of big data – combine unique and esoteric skills. Jonathan Goldman, who administered the data science team behind LinkedIn's highly successful "People You May Know" button, says data scientists are sometimes referred to as "unicorns" simply because the combination of skills and talents required to do their job is so rare and hard to find.

The old traditional market-research skills don't cut it in data science. The practitioners of this new art of research must be able to detect and make sense out of patterns hidden within millions upon millions of pieces of constantly streaming, completely unstructured data. They also must be able to smooth and clean the data, ask the right questions about that data, make valid inferences from the data as to how consumers and markets behave, and finally, create statistical models with which to pinpoint behavioral triggers which prove or disprove their theories.

These professionals come from almost all realms of learning, except – ironically – business schools.

At the Etsy e-commerce firm, we find at work a biostatistics Ph.D. who after a decade of mining medical databases for therapeutic data, now spends her days creating statistical models to figure out the terms people use when they search Etsy from their smart phones for a new fashion they've just seen on the street. At Yelp, a man with a doctorate in applied mathematics has taken his dissertation research on genome-mapping and transitioned it for use to measure how numerous small changes in online advertisements impact consumer behavior.

"Academia is slow and only a few people see your work," says Scott Clark, designer of the genome-mapping algorithm. "At Yelp, I can be pushing out experiments that affect hundreds of millions of people. When I make a small change to the Yelp website, I have a bigger impact."

Data sceince candidates with the right skill-sets routinely start in at six figure salaries, and most are earning between $200,000 and $300,000 after just a couple of years in the field. Josh Sullivan, the leader of a 500-person data science group at Booz Allen Hamilton, notes that anyone with "data science" on her or his LinkedIn profile will invariably get one hundred or more recruiter e-mails per day.

As usual, scarcity makes and defines the market. And when it comes to data scientists, the world has a great and growing scarcity. A random check of LinkedIn as I sit here writing shows more than 32,000 data science positions open, and unfilled. Per the consulting firm McKinsey, the United States will, by 2018, be suffering a shortage of 190,000 skilled data scientists as well as some 1.5 million analysts and managers skilled at harvesting useful and actionaable BI from the growing data deluge. The implications of this situation become obvious when one realizes by 2020 an annual average of 40,000 exabytes of data will be created annually, up from a mere 2700 exabytes in 2012.

According to the National Science Foundation, most data scientists are drawn from doctorate graduates in statistics, biostatistics, particle physics and computer science. But in 2012, only about 2,500 doctorate degrees in these fields were awarded nationwide across the United States. At the same time, the need for data science professionals continues to increase exponentially, along with the practice of the science itself. To try to sate business's ravenous appetite for talent, numerous universities have now launched, or are about to launch, data science certificate and master's programs. Other initiatives include the Insight Data Science Fellows Program, with locations near Stanford University and also Manhattan, which has been funded by various tech companies to facilitate the transition of doctoral candidates in math, astrophysics and neuroscience to data science.

Data science is not a tough sell to these young men and women. The lure is not hard to understand. Grants for pure scientific research are few and far between. So, too, are tenure track teaching and researching positions in academia. For the longest time, the only other option for a statistically-minded young person would be to a become quantitative analyst on Wall Street. But now, data science is there, offering great remuneration and, almost as important, intellectually-challenging research.

An example: An astrophysicist employed as a data scientist at TaskRabbit – a firm that helps individuals and business employers find part-time and short-time workers (aka "rabbits") for basic chores like packing boxes or power-washing boats or housekeeping – spent half a year creating complex algorithms for a data model which incorporates a worker's geographical location, experience, payment rate, available hours, and ratings by past employers to match that worker to a new employer posting a job. Over time, the software learns to weight these attributes and "discover" which factors are of most importance to would-be employers. In this, the astrophysicist uses the same skills she would in order to test new theories in particle physics. But she now her work is less esoteric and more meaningful in the real world. "At the end of the day, who you choose to show isn't just a listing," she says. "It's something that directly affects people's livelihoods."

2

Part Analyst,
Part Inspired Artist

The intuitive mind is a sacred gift and the rational mind is a faithful servant. We have created a society that honors the servant and has forgotten the gift. ... More than anything else, this new century demands new thinking: We must change our materially based analyses of the world around us to include broader, more multidimensional perspectives.
- Albert Einstein

One of the key things separating a data scientist from a standard traditional business or data analyst is the need for the data scientist to look at the data, *lots* of data, much of it unstructured, and use *great intuitive leaps* to devise methods and approaches for gaining the best actionable BI. Thus imagination and inspiration are called for, along with the ability to figure out the right questions to ask of the data. It is a simple thing to mine a lot of useless facts from data. The key is to ask the right questions and thus gain the most *useful* facts. And asking the right questions involves imagination

For this reason, data scientists have sometimes been described as "part analyst, part artist." According to Anjul Bhambhri, IBM's VP of big data products, a data scientist "is somebody who is inquisitive, who can stare at data and spot trends. It's almost like a Renaissance individual who really wants to learn and bring change ..." A data scientist is charged with looking at data from many angles. In fact, not only is the data scientist *required* to look at data from many different angles, he or she is responsible for isolating those particular angles of vision which will yield the best results.

In short, data scientists must be always exploring, always asking new and original questions, always doing "what if" analyses, always questioning and testing current assumptions, methods and processes. The data scientist's role is one of both invention and reinvention, discovery and rediscovery, imagining and reimagining. The data scientist believes rules are there to be tested and revised, established knowledge there to be overthrown, and systems of belief there to be re-architected. The popular term *disruption* comes to mind. The mission of the data scientist is to *discover new information*, powerful information with the potential to radically and drastically change thinking, approaches, habits, methodologies and profitability. If some order of significant change and improvement is not the result of his or her efforts, then the data scientist is not doing his or her job.

Speaking about his researches into physics, Albert Einstein once commented: "There is no logical way to the discovery of these elemental laws. There is only the way of *intuition*, which is helped by a *feeling* for the order lying behind the appearance." Jonas Salk, discoverer of the polio vaccine, said something similar when he claimed: "Intuition will tell the thinking mind where to look next."

Industry pundit Stan Gibson insists the best data scientist will be one inclined to "crunch a hunch." In other words, to start with an intuited theory, and then work the data to prove or disprove that theory. "You have to have an idea of what you are looking for," he writes. "What do you want to find? Why? What will you do with it if it's there?"

Gibson continues: "If you have read either *Freakonomics* or *Super Freakonomics*, by Steven Levitt and Stephen Dubner, you have been exposed to the importance of intuiting the right questions. Levitt, with a relentlessly inquisitive mind, looks at seemingly obvious facts, suspects that all may not be as it appears, and then launches a quest to learn more. More often than not, he discovers a counter-intuitive truth."

New York Times tech correspondent Steve Lohr thinks intuition the largest part of the process. "My…concern," he writes, "is that the algorithms … shaping my digital world are too simple-minded, rather than too smart. It's encouraging that thoughtful data scientists … recognize the limits and shortcomings of the big data technology … they are building. Listening to the data is important … but so is experience and intuition. After all, what is intuition at its best but large amounts of data of all kinds filtered through a human brain rather than a math model?"

Industry pundit John Weathington calls the best data scientists "visionary strategists." "The inputs to their decision-making process are inferential and aggregated, unlike their counterparts who use purely sensory data. … [They] make decisions through a logical, rational, thinking process. They do care what other people think, yet everything must pass the logic test before it makes sense. …" They are intellectually independent. They are comfortable with swimming against the tide and voicing possible outcomes – theories others at the conference table perhaps won't like. They delight in spotting outlier information which they believe may prove influential. To destroy a cliché, they not only think "outside" the box, but whenever they can they take an ax to the box and then set the broken shards on fire.

Noted data scientist Peter Skomoroch states emphatically and categorically that intuition and creativity are essential to the field. He points out that "companies with the courage to get behind the intuition of data scientists – without a lot of evidence yet that their ideas will be successful – will be the ones [to] develop successful" results. "As with traditional analytics … you will have to eventually test your creativity with data and analysis." But the payoff can, and often will, be enormous in the way of guidance toward innovation.

3
Data Wrangling

The goal is to turn data into information, and information into insight.
- Carly Fiorina

As intellectually stimulating as the work might be, there are also mundane aspects to the data scientist's job. In fact, there is pure drudge work that can take from 50 to 80 percent of a data scientist's time. This involves the collecting, cleaning and organizing of unruly, disparate, messy, unstructured data before it can be mined for the gold of actionable BI. Some call this aspect of the job "data wrangling."

Monica Rogati serves as data science VP at Jawbone, a firm marketing a sensor-packed wristband designed to track the food purchases, sleep habits, and like personal attributes in order to make suggestions as to recommended dietary changes and exercise regimens. "Data wrangling is a huge – and surprisingly so – part of the job," she says. "It's something that is not appreciated by data civilians. At times, it feels like everything we do."

Del Monte Foods CIO Tim Weaver describes data wrangling as big data's "iceberg" issue. All most laymen see of data science is the 20% floating at the surface in the form of beautiful, elegant and profitable BI. They don't realize the 80% of sheer tedium looming underwater.

One of the most robust and powerful aspects of big data is, of course, the opportunity it provides to combine disparate data sets in order to triangulate otherwise unobtainable key information and rubrics. But in this opportunity lies also the most grueling fundamental headache of data science. Raw data from different sources and different devices comes in many different formats. All of this must be cleaned and coalesced into one standard format upon which an algorithm can perform its task.

Different data packages from different data collectors often use different terms to define common points of data, and use different parameters to quantify common quantities. A "core unit" in one data set may be the exact same item as a "base unit" in another. The number "10" in one data set might refer to meters, while the same numeral in another data set might equate to miles. It takes pure, menial, human intervention to render these disparate data sets uniform before an algorithm, unable to cope with such subtleties, can effectively be turned loose. As Iodine co-founder and data scientist Matt Mohebbi puts it, there is simply no way to "get to the cool, sexy things that got you into the field in the first place," without biting the bullet, digging in, and doing the grunt-work. "We really need better tools," says Ford Motor data scientist Michael Cavaretta, "so we can spend less time on data wrangling and get to the sexy stuff."

Most industry-watchers and pundits expect the time needed for data wrangling to shrink and condense as we move forward. Slowly, software implementations are being developed which streamline and automate the process. For example, the Palo Alto start-up ClearStory Data creates software designed to interpret many different data formats and sources, smooth these, and present the results in understandable graphical charts and/or data-filled maps. Each visual is usually the result of combining six to eight sources of data. A presentation for a retailer might combine web traffic diagnostics, point-of-sale records, pricing data, results of parking lot video tracking, and data gathered from visits to the retailer's smartphone app.

Another firm, Trifacta, distributes software which employs machine-learning methodologies to discover, present and recommend data sources and approaches that might be useful to a given data scientist working on a given data project. Joseph Hellerstein, chief strategy officer at Trifacta and computer science professor at the University of California, Berkeley, says: "We want to lift the burden from the user, reduce the time spent on data preparation."

The Redwood City start-up Paxata, has likewise focused on the automation of data preparation. Their software greatly speeds the process of discovering, cleaning and combining data into an easily analyzed and navigated data set – one designed to seamlessly integrate with a wide range of analysis and visualization tools.

4
The Human Factor
vs. The Machine Factor

In God we trust. All others must bring data.
- W. Edwards Deming, statistician, professor, author,
lecturer, and consultant

But some things simply can't be automated. Such things as nuance, instinct, intuition and common sense are – at least so far – uniquely human attributes not teachable to any machine and unlikely ever to be embraced by any algorithm. The extent to which human capabilities are needed depends on the nature of the data and the nature of the questions being imposed upon that data. Thus, while some some data scientists are tasked with preparing data for machines to interpret, others find themselves more focused on preparing data for humans to interpret.

When the final consumer of analysis, and the decision maker, is to be a computer (such as might be the case with algorithmic stock trading, automated product recommendations, or the targeting of content), the data scientist's task is to build extremely complex models capable of swallowing enormous data sets and then extracting the most subtle flags and signals via robust algorithms and machine-learning software tools. What's created are digital models designed to make and execute decisions on their own initiative, making recommendations to shoppers, delineating which ads to display to a given user, issuing buy and sell orders on stocks, and so on.

The data scientists charged with preparing analysis for computers need to be particularly strong in their mathematical, computational and statistical skills. 90% of their time is taken up working with clear, in-arbitrary metrics – in other words, solid data precisely quantifying clicks, purchases, profits and so forth – and using these to build data models designed to drive performance and increase revenue.

When the ultimate decision maker consuming analysis is to be human, a different data science skill-set comes into play. Data scientists need to be less obtuse in their approach to modeling. The results of their research, and the resulting BI, have to be *understandable* to decision makers residing behind desks rather than inside cyberspace. This data scientist must be capable of understanding the subtle relationship between marketing, pricing and products ... relating to the nuances of user attitudes and retention ... producing effective presentations and reports.

This data scientist still works with enormous data sets, but unlike the scientist working only with and for machines, he or she must understand how to conceptualize and tell a story from that data. She or he has to be able to summarize, back-up and explain results and recommendations. These data scientists often have to use, for the sake of their clients' understanding, simpler data models rather than more complex data models, no matter how much added pinpoint accuracy might be obtained with the latter. They also have to be competent to impose their own interpretations onto the data results, providing reasoning the machine cannot: the *how* and *why* of the story.

The ideal background for a data scientist generating analytics for machines would be an advanced degree in engineering, the natural sciences or mathematics. These are professionals with a deep computational and mathematical knowledge-base, this enabling them to engage the highest-level and most complex modeling paradigms.

Such a person, however, is likely to be a disaster when it comes to generating analytics for human consumption. For this task, economists and social scientists, although generally possessed of slightly lower skills when it comes to modeling, are often ideal. This realm not only doesn't need highly-complex modeling, but generally eschews it. It does, however, demand intellectual reasoning: a professional capable of interpreting and explaining data in real-world terms.

It is a rare situation when one data scientist will possess all the skills necessary to accomplish every aspect of a project. The industry might well be calling for people who, as the saying goes, "can do it all." But the fact is these are not only unicorns, but unicorns who were never born. Data scientists tend to be talented and versed in three very different and distinct areas, or layers, and thus often work in teams.

The foundational infrastructure layer is and should be the realm of the data engineer. The next layer up, the algorithm layer, is and should be the realm of the data programmer: the elegant maker of models. And the third, top "decision science" layer is and should be the realm of business analysts interpreting and visualizing BI, in instances where this is the aim, for decision makers behind desks. Thus, the most sensible and pragmatic approach to most data science tasks is to form a team, each member of which has his or her own particular strength. But overall, according to one expert, the top quality which managers should insist upon in *any* data scientist working at *any* level is curiosity and a willingness to "play with data and experiment with it and have lots of perseverance."

5

The Data Scientist's
Shifting Role

The psychological profiling [of a programmer] is mostly the ability to shift levels of abstraction, from low level to high level. To see something in the small and to see something in the large.
- Donald Knuth

Anant Jhingran, one of the lead developers of IBM's famous WATSON, despises the term *data scientist*.

Jhingran suggests the term creates an aura which implies data scientists are "inapproachable" and every aspect of their black magic unreproducible by software. He also believes the term gives software developers an "easy out" by suggesting big data is "very fickle and working with it is hard." Therefore they can say: "Let's not bother with it. Let's not build apps that learn and understand and change." Jhingran believes the term performs a disservice to both sides – sides between which there should be no gap, sides which need not be opposed.

Jhingran insists the data scientist must learn to "think like a developer"as the capability to access and leverage big data comes more into the mainstream of the enterprise. In time, he says, data scientists are destined to become less like "magicians operating behind a curtain," and instead work hand-in-glove with the developer community to create value for end-users. Calling developers "the new kingmakers," Jhingran explains "they are unlocking business value by building apps. The data scientist needs to have a new mindset – it's not just about solving big problems in isolation anymore. The mindset has to be: *How do I enable these developers?"*

At Jhingran's current home, Apigee, he places data scientists within developer teams. Jhingran says he makes "data scientists actually sit in the teams that it is their job to enable. They live and breathe their problems. That has made a big difference in the data scientists' understanding that their job is to enable people to succeed."

In the Apigee environment, the data scientists now create their data models in such a way as to be readily accessible by APIs – Applications Programming Interfaces – which developers can use to maximize their apps. According to Jhingran, "All that happens because the data scientists have not just done the hard work on difficult problems, but gone the next mile to enable developers."

Conversely, developers have to change their cultural mindset as well.

Says Jhingran: "Developers have typically thought of themselves as programming either the user interface or the app or the business logic. Whenever they talk about 'data,' they talk about data as persistent as opposed to data as analytics. It's not that they don't get it, it's just that it has always been difficult. We strongly believe that the developer of the future will not be a single-skill developer. Being able to play with data needs to become a very, very important developer skill."

In short, the software developer of the future will have to be one-part developer and one-part data scientist, as comfortable playing with data as he or she is with business logic of user interface logic.

6

A Cool Sub-Niche:
Crowd Science

Men, it has been well said, think in herds; it will be seen that they go mad in herds, while they only recover their senses slowly, one by one.
- Charles Mackay

One of the most interesting categories of data science is the emerging field of crowd science, an arcane specialty residing at the intersection of analytics and psychology. (Note: This is not to be confused with another altogether different discipline also called *crowd science,* that of crowd-sourced scientific projects.)

Practitioners of crowd science as practiced in the data science community apply standard data science techniques – techniques such as statistical modeling, data mining and algorithm creation – to all manner of crowd-sourced data, such as that derived from activity on social networks. By focusing on human interactions taking place within the digital space, crowd science enables the gathering of BI with regard to behavioral and psychological traits, and the varying habits of people in target-markets. In this, the data scientist's focus is on how people relate to each other in various social structures, how they influence and learn from each other, how ideas and opinions travel through social networks, what inspires people to chime in on discussions, and other such nebulous questions. In short, the data scientist is looking at the mechanics and dynamics of crowd mentality, opinion and action.

MIT's Alex Pentland eschews the term "crowd science" in favor of another: *social physics*. Dr. Pentland defines this as "a quantitative social science that describes reliable, mathematical connections between information and idea flow on the one hand and people's behavior on the other. Social physics helps us understand how ideas flow from person to person through the mechanism of social learning and how this flow of ideas ends up shaping the norms, productivity, and creative output of our companies, cities and societies."

Crowd science is ubiquitous. It is everywhere. It is at the heart of research into shaping user experience in a range of online platforms and products. If you have ever had Amazon recommend a book to you based on purchase by others with whom you share certain buying habits, you've benefited from crowd science. If you've ever clicked on a Twitter "trending" link, you've benefited from crowd science. If you've ever employed or deployed a hashtag, you've engaged in the exploitation of crowd science.

But there is a dark side to crowd science. In order to gather the data necessary to forecast crowd behavior, it is necessary for the "crowd scientist" to use members of the crowd as lab rats – or, if you prefer, rhesus monkeys. There are few who don't remember the outrage voiced by Facebook users after they learned Facebook data scientists had manipulated their news feeds while conducting a behavioral experiment.

Explaining the fundamental difference between standard data science and crowd science, Mindjet data scientist Anna Gordon explains that while both involve finding signals and patterns in large amounts of noisy unstructured data, "crowd science explores data that has a subjective element to it: the psychology, variable behaviors, and opinions of the crowd. This begets a different kind of noise from what the typical data scientist must filter out. Members of a crowd can have vastly different opinions about a topic, might accidentally or intentionally enter incorrect data, or might try to outsmart the system. As a result, crowd scientists must eliminate outlying data points and introduce techniques that ensure honesty."

The nuances in crowd science are myriad. The challenges great. The possibilities fascinating.

7
The Data Scientist's Most Important Tool: Hadoop

Always code as if the guy who ends up maintaining your code will be a violent psychopath who knows where you live
- Martin Golding

Of course, what lies at the heart of big data is the ability to exercise real-time high performance data science in order to gain insight into the behavior of customers, markets, business partners, users, etc. Enormous growth in the amount of information businesses must track has greatly challenged legacy database platforms. Current unstructured and text-centric data sources, such as Facebook and Twitter feeds, categorically do not fit into yesterday's "structured" data model. Unstructured data-sets are by definition very big, sloppy and difficult to work with. They require radically new tools and solutions. The software platform Hadoop provides an essential solution, and thus has become the most important item in every data scientist's toolkit.

Hadoop is a free, Java-based programming tool for processing massive data sets in a distributed environment. The tool comes from the non-profit Apache Software Foundation. As shall be delineated later in this book, the powerful but sometimes-unwieldy Hadoop can be brought to heel and made easily manageable by a range of tools, including proprietary Hadoop implementations offered by major providers catering to the big data needs of various enterprises.

An open source product, Hadoop has rapidly become the dominant platform for big data analytics. Hadoop's principal characteristics are: scalability, flexibility, and economy. Thus it has become vital for enterprises confronted with such issues as extensive click-stream analysis as well as ad targeting. Numerous enterprises who have heretofore been struggling with the limitations of traditional database platforms are now rushing to employ Hadoop in their data analysis scenarios. (These industries are also looking for economy. According to a recent report from Infineta Systems, an impressive start-up concerned with Wide-Area-Network (or WAN) optimization, traditional data storage runs on average $5 per gigabyte, while with Hadoop the storage of identical data costs just 25 cents per gigabyte.)

Writing for *InformationWeek*, Doug Henschen tells us: "Excitement around Hadoop has been building since its release as an open source distributed data processing platform [several] years ago. [The platform] has taken off, gaining customers, commercial support options, and dozens of integrations from database and data-integration software vendors. The top three commercial database suppliers – Oracle, IBM, and Microsoft – have adopted Hadoop. ... Will Hadoop turn out to be as significant as Structured Query Language (or SQL), introduced more than 30 years ago? Hadoop is often tagged as a technology exclusively for unstructured data. By combining scalability, flexibility, and low cost, it has become the default choice for web giants like AOL and ComScore that are dealing with large-scale clickstream analysis and ad targeting scenarios."

Hadoop is, quite simply, all over the place. Facebook, Yelp, Etsy, eBay and Salesforce are just a few of the franchises which use Hadoop as their key tool for harvesting, cleaning, digesting and analyzing the massive flood of data generated by their millions of customers and users every minute of every day.

Henschen continues: "Hadoop is headed for [even] wider use. It's applicable for all types of data and destined to go beyond clickstream and sentiment analysis. For example, SunGard, a hosting and application service provider for small and midsize companies, plans to introduce a cloud-based managed service aimed at helping financial services companies experiment with Hadoop-based MapReduce processing. And software-as-a-service startup Tidemark recently introduced a cloud-based performance management application that will use MapReduce to bring mixed data sources into product and financial planning scenarios."

A study by Allied Market Research predicts Hadoop and related software, hardware and services will represent a software market of approximately $50.2 billion in 2020 (this indicating an annual growth rate of some 58% over the previous seven years).

Another respected analyst, Jeff Kelley, writes: "The market is being driven by the growing enterprise demand for more flexible, scalable and affordable data management solutions (both analytical and transactional) than currently offered by the relational database management market, which is dominated by Oracle, and the data warehouse market (itself a sub-segment of the RDBMS market), the traditional stronghold of Teradata."

Hadoop's origins lay in several early implementations, most importantly Google's *MapReduce.* The MapReduce program was designed to take an application and break it down into very small parts (sometimes called *fragments* or *blocks*). In turn, any one of these parts can be run on any node in a cluster. Hadoop extends this, empowering enterprises to run applications on systems with literally thousands of nodes embracing thousands of terabytes at one time.

Such a distributed file system (or DFS) creates very fast data transfer rates amid nodes, and empowers the system to continue operating without any perceptible interruption in case of a node failure. Thus the risk of overall catastrophic system failure is negligible even if a large number of nodes fail at once. "The Hadoop platform was designed to solve problems where you have a lot of data — perhaps a mixture of complex and structured data — and it doesn't fit nicely into tables," says Cloudera CEO Mike Olson. "It's for situations where you want to run analytics that are deep and computationally extensive, like clustering and targeting. That's exactly what Google was doing when it was indexing the web and examining user behavior to improve performance algorithms."

The platform is architected to run on a large number of machines. Says Olson: "That means you can buy a whole bunch of commodity servers, slap them in a rack, and run the Hadoop software on each one. When you want to load all of your organization's data into Hadoop, what the software does is bust that data into pieces." Then it spreads all those pieces across your various servers. "There's no one place where you go to talk to all of your data; Hadoop keeps track of where the data resides. And because there are multiple copy stores, data stored on a server that goes offline or dies can be automatically replicated from a known good copy."

In the case of a traditional centralized database, you are working with one large disk usually linked to from four to 16 robust processors. "But that is as much horsepower as you can bring to bear," says Olson. "In a Hadoop cluster, every one of those servers has two or four or eight CPUs. You can run your indexing job by sending your code to each of the dozens of servers in your cluster, and each server operates on its own little piece of the data. Results are then delivered back to you in a unified whole. That's MapReduce: you map the operation out to all of those servers and then you reduce the results back into a single result set. ... [The] reason you're able to ask complicated computational questions is because you've got all of these processors, working in parallel, harnessed together."

Hadoop has been deployed by such major players as Google, Yahoo and IBM, largely for applications concerned with targeted advertising and search engines. Although preferred the operating systems are Windows and Linux, Hadoop can nevertheless perform well with BSD and OS X.

"Facebook uses Hadoop ... extensively to process large data sets," notes Ashish Thusoo, Engineering Manager at Facebook. The firm deploys Hadoop to handle a number of important tasks such as index generation, adhoc analysis, etc. By necessity, Facebook works with one of the world's largest clusters: 23000 cores, 20 petabytes. The firm also deploys Hadoop (and Scribe) in the process of log collection – to the tune of 50 terrabytes of raw data each and every day.

Hadoop is also key to the processing at LinkedIn and Twitter. Hadoop allows both these entities to collect, mine, perform analysis on, and produce highly useful intelligence from data in real-time. "We are excited about the rate of progress that Hadoop is achieving, and will continue our contributions to its thriving open source community," notes Kevin Weil, Twitter's Analytics Lead.

Then we have eBay. Back in 2010, eBay built a Hadoop cluster embracing no less than 530 servers. But within one year, that cluster had grown by a factor of five. The firm uses this computing power to do everything from analyzing inventory information to creating profiles of individual customers via the study of real-time behavior.

8
A Fantastic
Kind of Abstraction:
The Origins of Hadoop

Abstraction can provide stumbling blocks for people of strange intelligence.

- Gustave Flaubert

We can trace the origins of Hadoop back to 2002. In that year, the Internet Archive's Doug Cutting together with a graduate student (Mike Cafarella from Washington State University) set out to build an open source search engine they called *Nutch*. The idea was to be able to quickly crawl and process Internet data in what *was then* a great volume: several hundred million web pages. In retrospect, Nutch had a number of limitations which were bound to become crippling as the size and rate of data grew. First of all, it could only be run across a few machines at one time. As well, it was so unstable that human-eyes had to be on it 24-7 to make sure it didn't crash.

"I remember being quite proud of what we had been doing ..." notes Cafarella. "[But] then the Google File System paper came out [in October 2003] and I realized: 'Oh, that's a much better way of doing it ...' Then, by the time we had a first working version, the MapReduce paper came out [in December 2004] and that seemed like a pretty good idea too."

Per Mike Olson: Hadoop's underlying technology "was invented by Google back in their earlier days so they could usefully index all the rich textural and structural information they were collecting, and then present meaningful and actionable results to users." Google's paper described a distributed scalable file system for very large, data-intensive, distributed applications. Requiring only highly-economical hardware, the system delivered robust fault-tolerance and very high-aggregate performance across many machines.

Of most importance was the scalability: the capability to remain reliable as data grew in volume, and as the number of machines involved increased. At the time the paper was presented, the system was already in use at Google. The firm's largest cluster delivered many hundreds of terabytes of storage on thousands of disks scattered across thousands of machines. The Google File System paper was delivered at the 19th ACM Symposium on Operating System Principles held at Lake George, New York in October of 2003. The paper was authored by Sanjay Ghemawat, Howard Gobioff and Shun-Tak Leung.

Presented the following year and authored by Sanjay Ghemawat and Jeffrey Dean, Google's MapReduce paper described an elegant and radically-new programming model together with a superior implementation for creating and processing very large data sets. Within MapReduce, users defined map functions for the process of a key/value pair, this in turn generating a set of key/value pairs together with a reduce function that merged intermediate values merged with the same intermediate key.

"Programs written in this functional style are automatically parallelized and executed on a large cluster of commodity machines," wrote the authors. "The run-time system takes care of the details of partitioning the input data, scheduling the program's execution across a set of machines, handling machine failures, and managing the required inter-machine communication. This allows programmers without any experience with parallel and distributed systems to easily utilize the resources of a large distributed system. Our implementation of MapReduce runs on a large cluster of commodity machines and is highly scalable: a typical MapReduce computation processes many terabytes of data on thousands of machines. Programmers find the system easy to use: hundreds of MapReduce programs have been implemented and upwards of one thousand MapReduce jobs are executed on Google's clusters every day."

This paper was presented at OSDI '04: The Sixth Symposium on Operating System Design and Implementation, held in San Francisco in December of 2004.

MapReduce signaled a revolution. Looking back, Raymie Stata, former Yahoo Chief Technology Officer (CTO) and founder of the Hadoop startup VertiCloud, recalls MapReduce as a "fantastic kind of abstraction" over the heretofore common distributed computing procedures and algorithms. "Everyone had something that pretty much was like MapReduce because we were all solving the same problems. We were trying to handle literally billions of web pages on machines that are probably, if you go back and check, epsilon more powerful than today's cell phones. ... So there was no option but to latch hundreds to thousands of machines together to build the index. So it was out of desperation that MapReduce was invented."

In June 2014, ten years after the birth of MapReduce, Google execs at the Google I/O Developers Conference introduced Cloud Dataflow, which they said would replace MapReduce, the latter, though robust in its prime, now being "so 2004-ish." MapReduce is "batch oriented, when what you really need is a system that can handle both a large amount of data set aside for a scheduled batch process and one that can handle an ad hoc stream of unsorted data." So writes industry analyst Charles Babcock. With Cloud Dataflow deployed on Google Apps Engine or Compute Engine, data scientists can still do batch processing but also handle real-time streaming data. Thus does Google MapReduce go into retirement after worthy service, its work done.

But now, for our purposes, let's get back to the ancient days of 2004 and the revolution engendered by that newborn named *MapReduce*.

9
A Platform
is Born

*People think that computer science is the art of geniuses but the actual
reality is the opposite, just many people doing things that build on
each other, like a wall of mini stones.*
- Donald Knuth

In the months following the presentation of the MapReduce
paper, Cutting and Cafarella began work on the fundamental
file systems and framework for processing that would
eventually be called *Hadoop*. Importantly, the two pioneers
worked using Java even though Google's MapReduce had been
implemented using C++. In turn, they layed Nutch across the
top of the framework.

Java, they correctly believed, offered the maximum
portability they sought in their platform, with its handy "write
once, run anywhere" adaptability and its convenient, rich array
of class libraries. It should be noted, however, that in recent
years some (though by no means *all*) technologists have
questioned the wisdom of this move, as an optimized C++
implementation would run just as well while at the same time
drawing less hardware capacity and related power. The trade-
off, of course, would be ease of portability.

In any event, Hadoop was implemented in Java.

Cutting joined Yahoo as an engineer in 2006, by which time
Cafarella had become an associate professor at the University of

Michigan. It was at this point that Cafarella effectively removed himself from commercial Hadoop development in favor of focusing on academics. (He now jokes that his father calls him the "Pete Best'" of big data, recalling the original Beatles drummer who was left behind while the band skyrocketed to international fame. Cafarella nevertheless continues to work on numerous Hadoop- and big data-related projects within the academic setting, and is more than content with his decision.)

At Yahoo, Cutting was charged with building open source solutions based on the Google File System and MapReduce paradigms. It was at this point that Hadoop (which he'd recently named rather randomly and spontaneously after his young son's toy elephant) became an open source project with the non-profit Apache Software Foundation. So far as Cutting was concerned, this seemed the ideal approach "because I was looking for more people to work on it, and people who had thousands of computers to run it on."

At this point, Hadoop – although showing great promise – was still quite an inefficient and clumsy implementation, by no means equipped to efficiently handle web-scale search, and big data was not yet even seriously envisioned as either a demand or a potential. Hortonworks CEO Eric Baldeschwieler: "The thing you gotta remember is at the time we started adopting it, the aspiration was definitely to rebuild Yahoo's web search infrastructure, but Hadoop only really worked on 5 to 20 nodes at that point, and it wasn't very performant, either."

Looking back, Raymie Stata talks about the "slow march" towards scalability. In fact, Hadoop development was nothing short of arduous, demanding invention and re-invention over and over again – constantly testing the ingenuity and engineering imagination of all who worked on it. "It was just an ongoing slog ... every factor of 2 or [even] 1.5 ... was serious engineering work."

Very slowly, as the Hadoop technology evolved over the course of several years, Yahoo rolled it out onto what engineers called a "research grid" for use by in-house practitioners of the craft which has since become known as "data science." At first, Hadoop was engineered to extend across several dozen nodes, then eventually several hundred.

Per Baldschwieler: "This very quickly kind of exploded and became our core mission, because what happened is the data scientists not only got interesting research results – what we had anticipated – but they also prototyped new applications and demonstrated that those applications could substantially improve Yahoo's search relevance or Yahoo's advertising revenue."

10
Hadoop Grows Up

Information is the oil of the 21st century, and analytics is the combustion engine.
- Peter Sondergaard

Once Hadoop began demonstrating its tangible business viability (round about 2007), a certain level of formality was necessarily adopted around the platform. Yahoo was running most of its business (just about every click/batch process and nearly all the financial transactions) through Hadoop by 2008.

Eventually Yahoo used Hadoop for the range of core tasks: hosting line-of-business applications, filtering for spam, and implementing user-specific personalization on individual Yahoo pages. All of this together demanded the creation of service level agreements, not to mention protocols to meet rigid Securities and Exchange Commission requirements with regard to security, seeing how Yahoo began to run all sponsored searches through Hadoop. It also demanded robust and constant growth.

By 2011 – in which year Yahoo created its subsidiary firm Hortonworks and spun off all further Hadoop development – Yahoo's Hadoop infrastructure represented no less than 42,000 nodes and many hundreds of petabytes of storage. Concurrent with all this, Hadoop remained a vibrant open source Apache project, with many individual developers coming up with a vast range of intriguing, robust innovations and solutions.

By far, Yahoo's most valuable contribution to the Hadoop platform was what Yahoo engineers dubbed the "Capacity Scheduler." This tool submits jobs in orderly queues, allocates a portion of resource capacity to each queue, allocates free resources to each queue beyond their total capacity, and assigns and enforces priority labels to the various queues.

Doug Cutting departed Yahoo in August of 2009 to join the start-up Cloudera, which had been founded by Christophe Bisciglia, Mike Olson, Jeff Hammerbacher and Amr Awadallah (the latter a former Yahoo engineering VP) one year earlier. Cloudera represented the very first commercial Hadoop enterprise, and it quickly became the port via which most corporate CIOs got their first look at the platform.

Already a favorite of such early adopters as the engineers at Facebook, Hadoop soon became the dominant subject amid the tech industry's constant buzz and chatter. The IT and business press routinely sang the praises of its great promise, this revolutionary approach that offered not only massive economies of scale, but also invaluable real-time BI of a type, quality and timeliness that had not heretofore even been imagined, never mind achieved.

Today the Apache project continues to spur brilliant innovation, while at the same time a number of top software and database firms – among them Amazon, Microsoft and Oracle – offer their own highly-intuitive, imminently-efficient and easy-to-use proprietary commercial variations on the theme.

Administering a massive distributed implementation such as Hadoop works with is an extremely complex operation. Most CIOs and corporate IT departments have neither the staff, staff-time or expertise to start from scratch and build a custom

Hadoop application and system. Thus a range of vendors have stepped into the marketplace offering robust, easy-to-implement and manage, turn-key Hadoop solutions for enterprises that want to get up and running as quickly, economically and safely as possible – without excessive costs and without unnecessary risk to data.

One of the most popular solutions is Amazon's Elastic MapReduce (Amazon EMR). This web service empowers developers, businesses, researchers and data scientists to easily and cost-effectively spin up a custom Hadoop implementation. Amazon EMR is based on a hosted Hadoop framework running on Amazon's robust web-scale infrastructure Amazon Elastic Compute Cloud (Amazon EC2), and utilizes the capacity of Amazon Simple Storage Service (Amazon S3). The combined products allow enterprises to flexibly use as much or as little capacity as they require at any given moment to perform data-intensive tasks related to information mining, web indexing, data warehousing, log file analysis, financial analysis, machine learning, scientific simulation, and other fields of endeavor. Firms using Amazon EMR include razorfish.

Microsoft offers HDInsight, a fully Apache-compatible Hadoop implementation. The product is available for Windows Server and on Microsoft's Windows Azure platform for Cloud Computing. In its turn, Oracle's Big Data Appliance incorporates Cloudera's elegant Hadoop implementation, and also includes an implementation of NoSQL, another solution for unstructured data. Other products include Google's Big Query, and a range of offerings from smaller vendors, with more being announced every day.

In the final analysis, Hadoop is here to stay and – in many ways – still in its childhood as a platform. Much promise remains. Much growth and development is yet to come. The platforms's capacity for increasingly *nuanced* sorting and cleaning of huge chunks of unstructured data will only become more robust with the innovation of additional tools and procedures under the Apache umbrella and through R&D at such firms as Yahoo, Amazon and Microsoft.

Just as our ability to work with unstructured real-time data has increased in several orders-of-magnitude over the past few years, so it will again in the years to come. It is, in fact, hard at this point to envision what may lay "beyond" Hadoop. It seems itself a frontier, one largely unexplored and under-exploited. So the real question is not what will be next for databases, but what will be next for Hadoop.

11
A Cautionary Summing Up

Reality leaves a lot to the imagination.
- John Lennon

As should be clear by now, the quality data scientist is, though not mythical like a unicorn, certainly a very rare bird. The complex and subtle mix of skills and talents that go into shaping such inspired innovators and maestros of information are combinations which it is impossible to force, or to impose through an academic program.

One can learn the rules and methods of statistics and data analysis. One can be taught the fine art of deploying and adapting Hadoop. One can be shown how to clean dirty data and render varying file formats into uniform data sets. One can be instructed on the whys and wherefores of real-time analysis.

But intuition? Creativity? Imagination? Inspiration? The capacity to not only explore, but to intuitively realize what direction of exploration might yield the best end-result? The capability to gaze across a giant field of random data, define and detect flags, and then visualize some vital new truth, some previously unimagined fact? The talent to define and pose just the right question on just the right data? These are native strengths, unteachable, unlearnable and ultimately unreproducible in a machine, just as they are, sadly, in most human beings.

Bottom line: The chief and most necessary, in fact indispensable, skill of every good data scientist is being a visionary, a discoverer, a pathfinder. This is the truth behind the static hype you encounter when you see the *Harvard Business Review* simplify and characterize data science the "sexiest job of the 21st century."

Imaginative dexterity, and a lack of intellectual restraint. That's what the good data scientist must have. To quote Madeleine L'Engle's words from *A Wrinkle in Time*: "Don't try to comprehend with your mind. Your minds are very limited. Use your intuition." It is also useful to remember what Malcolm Gladwell has to say in *Blink: The Power of Thinking Without Thinking*: "Insight is not a light-bulb that goes off inside our heads. It is a flickering candle that can easily be snuffed out."

The good data scientist can never be tied up to perceived and accepted knowledge. He or she must always be free to steer freely on a course toward the dim flickering candle of insight, navigating ever closer until that insight is clear and bright.

But with the vision must also come the ability to manipulate the data, tame the data, wander through the data, and *test* what one's gut is saying about the data. As Einstein wrote: "I believe in intuitions and inspirations. … I sometimes *feel* that I am right. I do not *know* that I am." The knowing, if there was to be a knowing, came only after Einstein's intuitive leap had been proven (or not) by his extensive working out of equations. The invention of the idea must be followed by the proof of the idea. Blaise Pascal once said, "dull minds are never either intuitive or mathematical." The mind of a data scientist must be both, and certainly never dull.

The good data scientist will be as happy to be proved wrong in his or her theory as to be proved right. For something is learned even by being proved wrong. When we discover that a trail leads nowhere, we have *learned* the trail should be abandoned forever, the possibility set aside in the trash. *The failure itself becomes useful and important data.* Our knowledge-base has expanded in a significant and productive way. As the Buddhists say: *All is learning.*

The good data scientist will also be one who is willing to recognize the limits of his or her field. As Stewart Pratt, director of data and analytics at SapientNitro – a data-focused brand agency – says: "When I speak about the humility of the modern data scientist, I'm referring to receptivity to [the fact that even though] big data can help us identify correlations we may have otherwise missed, … it isn't well-suited for helping us to understand causality or meaning."

Microsoft Research's Kate Crawford expressed a similar point of view in her keynote address delivered to the Strata Conference held in Santa Clara on February 28th, 2013. Crawford criticized what she calls "'data fundamentalism,' the notion that correlation always indicates causation, and that massive data sets and predictive analytics always reflect objective truth. … Can numbers actually speak for themselves? Sadly, they can't. Data and data sets are not objective; they are creations of human design. *We* give numbers their voice, draw inferences from them, and define their meaning through our interpretations. Hidden biases in both the collection and analysis stages present considerable risks, and are as important to the big data equation as the numbers themselves."

Ms. Crawford's solution is the fledgling art of what we've previously referred to here as *crowd science*. "In the near term," she says, "data scientists should take a page from social scientists, who have a long history of asking where the data they're working with comes from, what methods were used to gather and analyze it, and what cognitive biases they might bring to its interpretation. Longer term, we must ask how we can bring together big data approaches with small data studies – computational social science with traditional qualitative methods. We know that data insights can be found at multiple levels of granularity, and by combining methods such as ethnography with analytics, or conducting semi-structured interviews paired with information retrieval techniques, we can add depth to the data we collect. We get a much richer sense of the world when we ask people the why and the how not just the 'how many'." In other words, the aim should be three-dimensional information, three-dimensional knowledge, with causality and meaning included.

Writing in the *New York Times* on the topic "What Data Can't Do," David Brooks noteed data's several shortcomings one by one. First, data struggles with *the social*. It can count your clicks and your interactions with Facebook "friends" or topics, but it can quantify your passion for one friend over another, or one topic over another. Second, data struggles with *context*. "Human decisions are not discrete events,"writes Brooks. "They are embedded in sequences and contexts. The human brain has evolved to account for this reality. People are really good at telling stories that weave together multiple causes and multiple contexts. Data analysis is pretty bad at narrative and emergent thinking, and it cannot match the explanatory suppleness of even a mediocre novel."

Data also has the propensity to simply *create bigger haystacks*. With more and more data, we are bound to find more and more seemingly significant statistical correlations – most of them false. As Brooks tells us: "Falsity grows exponentially the more data we collect." The haystack increases in size, but the needle we are looking for grows not at all.

There are other shortcomings as well. For example, the nature of big data does not allow for data scientists to compare results between a defined sample and a control group. Further, while data science and big data allow us to isolate products and programs that are succeeding or failing *in the now*, it is practically useless in helping us predict the future popularity of new products or programs which may be slow to take-off because of lack of familiarity, or some similar issue, and are not performing particularly well *in the now*.

Finally, echoing Crawford, Brooks reminds us that *data obscures values*. In the end, there is actually no such thing as "raw data." All data has somewhere along the line, perhaps several times along the line, been structured based on someone's values, predispositions and biases. Subjective judgments are – and need to be – made again and again, all the way through the process. Nevertheless, they can hurt the outcome BI if not done correctly, and we must be mindful of this.

The largest part of the data scientist's task is to recognize and navigate these shortcomings, steering around these rocks and shoals, in order to make a successful voyage toward those truths which are most productive, actionable and profitable BI.

So endth this lesson.

About the Author

Lars Nielsen is a prominent IT consultant based in Amsterdam. His books include *Computing: A Business History* and *A Simple Introduction to Data Science,* both published by New Street.

newstreetcommunications.com